CATMANIA

IT'S SP

UK KENT

READING.

UCKY NIKE

DEDICATION

To BD with love.
Shannon

———————

To Ruth and Bert Morrison,
my parents, my mentors,
my technical advisors,
my heroes.
Love, Marc

———————

To
Richard Ernest Johnson
"Lewis"
(1919-1982)

and
Mary Louise Johnson
"Grams"
Grams, you are
and always will be
"the cat's meow"
to me.
Love, Karen

CATMANIA

SHANNON PARKS

Photography by
MARC MORRISON
KAREN WULFFRAAT

TRIUMPH
BOOKS
CHICAGO

Handmade stained glass by Amy & John Vucci, Tampa, Florida

SHANNON THANKS

William S. Parks, M.D., my dad, my friend, and my biggest fan; Bill Keightley, Brooks Downing, Kyle Moats, Sandy Boykin, and everyone else in the University of Kentucky athletic department for your support; Ireene and Tonny van der Leeden; Gerry Wood; Janis Christenson for helping keep the insanity to a minimum; and last but not least, Marc Morrison and Karen Wulffraat for the true beauty you put into every image.

MARC THANKS

Karen Wulffraat for your undying desire for perfection, your infinite pool of creativity, and for always being able to pull a bunny from your hat; Lisa Morrison who gets my vote for coach of the year; Troy Fields for keeping Karen awake and fed so she could finish this book, and for being a best friend. Joe Aker, Carl Champagne, and all of the great folks at AZ Lab for making us look great; Alice McKinney, Bruno Torres, Murray Getz, and Celeste Frisbee for your unconditional support through the years.

KAREN THANKS

Marc Morrison for daring to go on the road with two crazy chicks. You are my greatest teacher, my best friend, and the only visionary with the answer to my life's most important question . . . "Where are we going today, Pinky?" Carol and Leonard Wulffraat for Stephens College; Anne and Bill McBee (hats off to you and your great family and friends); Carl Champagne, my "Graphics Guru"; Richard Carson for shoving me in the general direction of a career; Connor Samuel for keeping my creativity charged and ready; RJ for patience and everything else.

Shannon, thanks for your gigantic imagination and your inability to comprehend the word no.

Printed in the United States of America

This book is available in quantity at special discounts for your group or organization. For more information, contact:
Triumph Books
601 South LaSalle Street
Suite 500
Chicago, Illinois 60605
(312) 939-3330
Fax (312) 663-3557

All photography by Photographers Morrison Wulffraat, except where noted.

ISBN 1-57243-346-9

7

FOREWORD

Since 1962, I've been blessed to serve as equipment manager in the "Capital of College Basketball"— the University of Kentucky. Having grown up in Lawrenceburg, not far from Lexington, I'm like most Kentuckians across this great state—a big fan of the Wildcats. And it's these fans who make this program what it is today: the most successful program in college basketball.

No other school can claim to have fans as dedicated as ours. The fans are the reason UK has developed this grand tradition, because they demand more from their team than any other fans at any other school. And the Cats are better because of it. There are fans who never miss a home game, and some who never miss games at all. We've had two streaks of a fan attending 600-plus games without a miss . . . we've had fans who have driven from Pikeville to Alaska to check out the Cats in action . . . we've even had groups of 100 fans who have traveled with the Cats overseas during summer tours.

It's a great thing to see the support in Rupp Arena, but it's amazing to see the swell of Big Blue fandom on the road. "Rupp Arena South" becomes a familiar slogan at nearly every Southeastern Conference Tournament, and at most NCAA Tournament sites. Opponents are amazed and intimidated by UK's crowd at most of these "neutral sites." March Madness is just that . . . madness. Cats fans are wild with enthusiasm at away games, and they often continue the cheering into the lobby of the team's hotel.

When one season ends, the countdown begins for Midnight Madness. Calls stream in, inquiring about the next season's schedule. Weddings are altered, babies are delivered, and vacations are planned around the Cats' schedule. The announcement of the schedule is the biggest off-season story each year. Simply stated, UK basketball thrives twenty-four hours a day, every day.

The tremendous success UK has achieved over the years—seven NCAA Championships and more wins than any other program in the nation—has developed a common bond among its followers. From the flatlands of Western Kentucky to the mountains of Eastern Kentucky, UK basketball brings together all walks of life. Since everyone enjoys being a part of something successful, the Wildcats are a source of pride for a rural state that has been long on desire but short on opportunities.

The fans' pride and enthusiasm in turn motivates the staff to work harder and the players to improve with each practice. They enjoy seeing the pleasure their hard work brings to their fans.

Wherever I go across the Bluegrass State, I come in contact with people who want to know about the Cats. This is a great honor for me, since I've never scored a point or coached a victory. I am just as big a fan as anyone else. Throughout my thirty-eight year tenure, I've worked for five different coaches—the only coaches we've had since 1930—and have had the pleasure of getting to know many of the great Wildcats who have worn the blue and white. So talking about the Cats is my favorite pastime.

Whether you live in Pikeville or Paducah, or in some other Big Blue outpost around the world, you will enjoy this book. *Catmania* explores the fanaticism of Kentucky basketball and the people who make it what it is today—a phenomenon.

So sit back and enjoy reading about the fans, their stories, and the excitement they create as they follow the Cats. I'm sure you'll have a few stories of your own to add as well. And remember, Go Big Blue!

So long,
Bill "Mr. Wildcat" Keightley
UK Equipment Manager

STICK IT TO 'EM, CATS

I take good care of my Wildcat fans. About eight years ago I started painting paws on my children when we would go to the games. I received so many compliments that I started doing face painting for other fans. Then I found a company that could make all of these little decals and tattoos, so that's what I use now. I go to all the football and basketball games plus the tournaments. I love my job.

"Tattoo" artist Kathy Bolton of Lexington, Kentucky, applies her art to Elea Soler of McDonough, Georgia

CAMERA CATS

I've been coming to the games
for about eighteen years. In New
Orleans I made national television
when I painted a #1 on my nose.
I still have the tape.

**Brooks "Hoot" Gibson (right),
Hazel, Kentucky, with Vicki Painter,
Loveland, Ohio**

Brooks "Hoot" Gibson,
Hazel, Kentucky

The Cats in back are Glenn Meadows, Keith Raglin, Anthony Adams, Wesley Graves, Steve Bale, Tony Pfuelb, & Steven Ford. In front are Linda Meadows, Cathy Bale, & Karen Ford. All are from Lexington, Kentucky.

A NIGHT TO REMEMBER

These ladies, all in their eighties, live in the same apartment building, on the same floor, and watch every Kentucky basketball game on TV. They decorate their doors, dress up, and serve refreshments at halftime. But they had never actually been to a game. So they wrote Tubby Smith a letter telling him that they were really big UK fans who never miss his games on TV. They also told him that they would like to see a game played at Rupp Arena before they died. So Tubby wrote back and told them they could come to the game of their choice that year. They chose the Vanderbilt game because it was Senior Night.

Jessica Parrish

We watch 'em all the time. We've been close friends for years. One game we'll go to Nellie's apartment, the next they'll all come over to mine. You'd think we were at the games the way we cut up. When we wrote to Tubby I thought he would just throw the letter away, but he didn't and here we are.

Lillian Romer

Lottie Mullins, Lillian Romer, Sandy Mullins, Nellie McNeil, & Jessica Parrish of Pikeville, Kentucky, enjoy the pregame festivities in the lobby of the Hyatt Regency Hotel before Kentucky played Vanderbilt University in Lexington, Kentucky.

HEAD FOR KENTUCKY

The Kentucky Wildcats are the best. There's no other team like them. I'm sixty-five years old and for as long as I can remember I've been a Wildcat fan. TV ruined some of our travel, but when it comes to championship games, we're there. Football? No, only round ball for me. Kentucky people just barely know how to spell "football," but we're learning.

**Jeanette Lindsey,
Paducah, Kentucky**

HAPPY CATS

Luke & Brock Jordan,
Paducah, Kentucky

GRANDFATHER CAT

I put two kids through the University of
Kentucky—undergraduate and graduate
school—so you'd better believe I'm a
Cats fan.

**Paul Binkley &
granddaughter Margaret,
Atlanta, Georgia**

PUTTING THE "WILD" IN WILDCATS

Dana McKnight, J. T. Fowler, Arlene Fowler, Robert McKinler, Lee New, Debbie Sutherland, Jane Gritton, & Mary Tejeda
put the "Wild" in Wildcats, New Orleans-style.

CUTE CAT

Abby Hughes,
Elizabethtown, Kentucky

BLUE BIRD

I was in a costume shop in Falls Church, Virginia, on New Year's Day, and I saw this hat and just had to have it. The lady who worked there said, "Are you going to Mardi Gras?" And I said, "Yes, Kentucky style!"

**Jack Grubbs,
Vine Grove, Kentucky**

CATS IN THE HATS

My wife Jennifer made this hat. She has more talent in her pinky than I have in my entire body. I have been a die-hard Kentucky basketball fan since day one.

**Larry Sandefur
Berea, Kentucky**

This hat goes way back. Actually, it's from Villanova's '84 championship, but I've fixed it up. It's better suited as a UK hat in my opinion.

**David Todd
Paint Lick, Kentucky**

**Joyce Ziegler & Jody Goode,
Florence, Kentucky**

BUTTON BUDDIES

I got the idea to make the vest from a girl who wore one to the Final Four in Seattle in 1984. I've been collecting buttons ever since. I always try to get extras to share with friends and to trade for the ones I don't have.

**Billie Sue Abbott (right),
Frankfort, Kentucky,
with Delores Weidemann,
Franklin, Kentucky**

BIG CAT, LITTLE CAT

**Jeffrey Baxter & daughter Allison,
Shreveport, Louisiana**

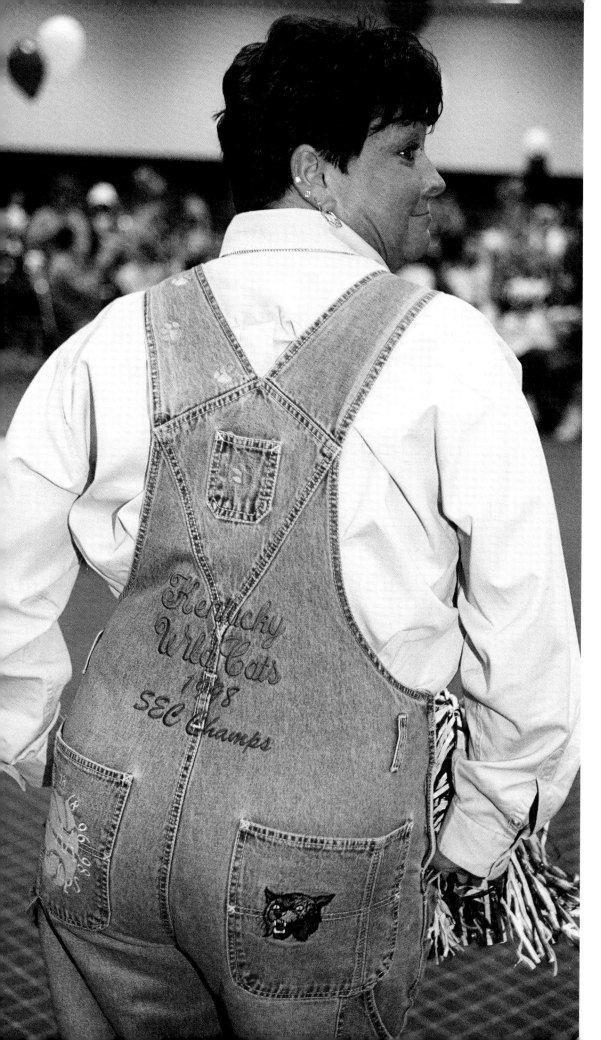

OVERALL BLUE

Underneath these things, my blood runs blue.

Sharon Wurth, Paducah, Kentucky

23

TRAVELLING CATS

All you have to do is go to
Greevey's Bar in Falls Church,
Virginia, anytime there's a
Kentucky game on TV—you are
guaranteed to see the whole restau-
rant filled with blue and white.

Cynthia Peffer, Washington, D.C.

**Included in her group are Dianne
& John DuPuy of Lexington,
Kentucky; Mary Ann Turner of Dallas,
Texas; & Phillip Nally of Lexington.**

BLUES BROTHER

I've been a Kentucky fan for almost forty years, and I've been listening to Cawood since I was an infant. My family bleeds blue. Kentucky basketball is the greatest thing to ever come into our lives. We listen to every game on the radio, watch every game that's televised, and when they are in the area, we go in person. I've got blue every-thing—guess you could say I've permanently got the blues.

Monty Hogan,
Mandeville, Louisiana

Monty Hogan, Mandeville, Louisiana, with family: Tim Hogan, Mandeville; Mark Greenberg, Covington, Louisiana; Jimmy Hogan, McComb, Mississippi; & Glen Hogan, Waveland, Mississippi.

RUNAWAY CAT FAN

I was getting ready to go to Myrtle Beach to see some family, but then I realized Kentucky was playing in New Orleans. So I thought that if I was going to drive ten hours to South Carolina, I might as well drive twelve hours and get to see the Cats play in the Superdome. So I went for it. I just took off, totally spur of the moment. When I got here I called my wife and said, "Uh, honey, the drive was fine but I'm in New Orleans, not Myrtle Beach."

**Stephen Wilkins,
Lexington, Kentucky**

ROAD DOGS

Jake travels with us to every game and is a huge Wildcat fan. He's very well known. I'll walk him around the stadium and everyone will say, "Hi, Jake." I mean everybody. Sunday is his favorite day during the football season because that's when all the RVs leave and he gets to eat their trash.

**Cheryl Glenn & Jake,
Frankfort, Kentucky**

All of our children are grown and away from home. So this is our new baby. We got Smoky at a pet store and yes, he was already named. We just hope it had absolutely nothing to do with the Tennessee Volunteers.

Billie Hollar & Smoky,
Frankfort, Kentucky

CAT CRUISERS

Going on the road allows many fans the opportunity to express their team spirit through their automobiles. Often decked out with everything from temporary decals and magnets to full-fledged paint jobs, these road cars are prized possessions, some of which never leave the garage except during peak season.

CAT CARRIER

Kentucky is so good, but the following makes it even better. It's such a group thing—everybody has fun. Plus it gets you away from work, and this beats the heck out of working.

**John B. DuPuy III,
Lexington, Kentucky**

Willa Itani,
Lexington, Kentucky

CAT CLOTHES

Dawahares has been outfitting Kentucky coaches for a long time, even back to Coach Rupp. I'm sure my Uncle Frank and my Uncle Willie sent brown suits to him. And then to Coach Hall. When Eddie Sutton came, we got a little attention. I remember Dick Vitale commenting on how well Coach Sutton was dressed. Dawahare's outfitted him exclusively. So when he left, we were already into making the coaches look good.

We were mostly using the Pierre Cardin line out of New York. When Coach Pitino was with the Knicks he already had a deal with Pierre Cardin, so when he came to Kentucky, we were excited because of the two connections. The coach of the University and Pierre Cardin. We received tremendous exposure because he was such a good model. Plus, we helped him look great.

We also work closely with Tubby. Before the first season even started we sat down with him and learned about his tastes, found out what he liked and didn't like. He's really easy to work with. Usually he wears whatever we pick out for him.

**Richard Dawahare,
Lexington, Kentucky**

A FAMILY BUSINESS

In addition to outfitting the coaches of the University of Kentucky, Dawahare's also carries a large selection of fan merchandise. Here, pictured left to right in front of a colorful blue and white display are family members Michael Dawahare, Mimi Dawahare, Joe Dawahare, A. F. Dawahare, Frank Dawahare Jr., Harding Dawahare, Richard Dawahare, and Joe Kawaja.

A TIE THAT BINDS

This tie just said, "Wildcats."
I live in Louisville but I grew up
in Portman and attended the
University of Kentucky, where I
earned my Ph.D. I am also only
one of one hundred people alive in
the Hall of Distinguished Alumni.
I attended my first Kentucky game
when they played Louisville in
Louisville. A friend of mine had
two tickets and asked if I wanted to
go. I was the only one in blue.

Jack Early,
Louisville, Kentucky

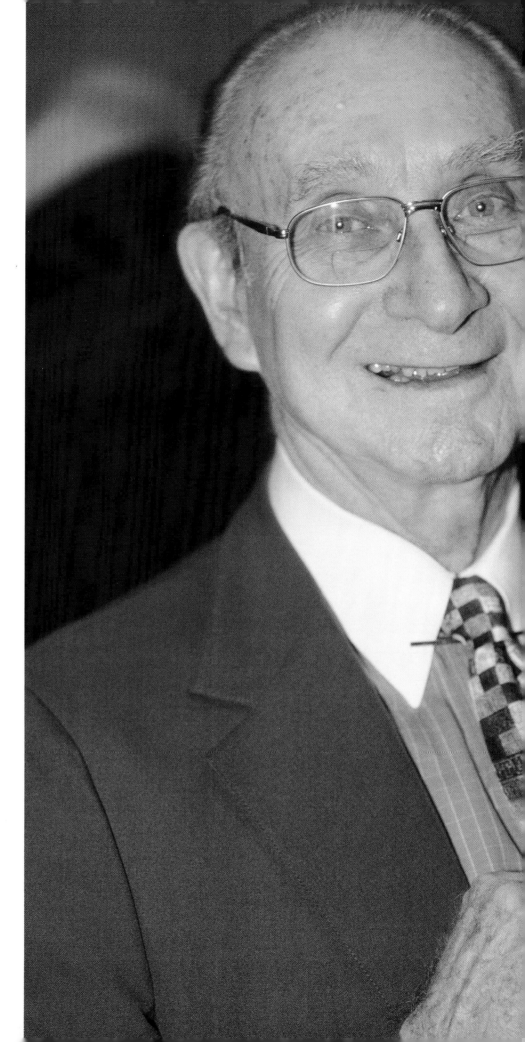

WILDCAT WEAR

No Cats fan can live without the latest blue and white souvenirs, grabbing up everything from championship yo-yos and frogs that croak the fight song to the standard jerseys, T-shirts, and ballcaps.

Jill & Dana Johnson,
Ashland, Kentucky

KENTUCKY KORNER

We started in 1982 with a small store in the Civic Center and now we have nine stores—two in Louisville, three in Lexington, and one each in Bowling Green, Ashland, and Florence. I've been here since the very first day. I was the first employee. The Wildcat fan is our business and we help them show their school spirit by providing all kinds of Kentucky merchandise. From the retail side, basketball season is fun for us, even if we do see it from a different angle. Unfortunately, we never get to go to the games because we're busy in the store, but we do experience the enthusiasm on game night almost as much. Kentucky Korner is a meeting place for many people actually going. They will eat dinner at the food court and then hang out in the store until tip-off. It's a social thing.

Phil Jeter,
Store Manager,
Kentucky Korner,
Lexington, Kentucky

Kentucky Korner,
Lexington, Kentucky

Rupp Arena, Lexington, Kentucky

Kelly Woods, Lexington, Kentucky, & Tracy Ullum &
Dave McNeely, Jefferson City, Tennessee

Lauren Wilson,
Danville, Kentucky

GIVE 'EM 3

I've been a Wildcat fan all of my life, and have been taking my kids to see the games since they were two years old.

Debra Ford with her triplets Hailey, Hunter, & Hilary Ford, Clay, Kentucky

PAINTED LADIES

Joyce Renfro,
Louisville, Kentucky, &
Jeanne Sheets,
Shelbyville, Kentucky

51

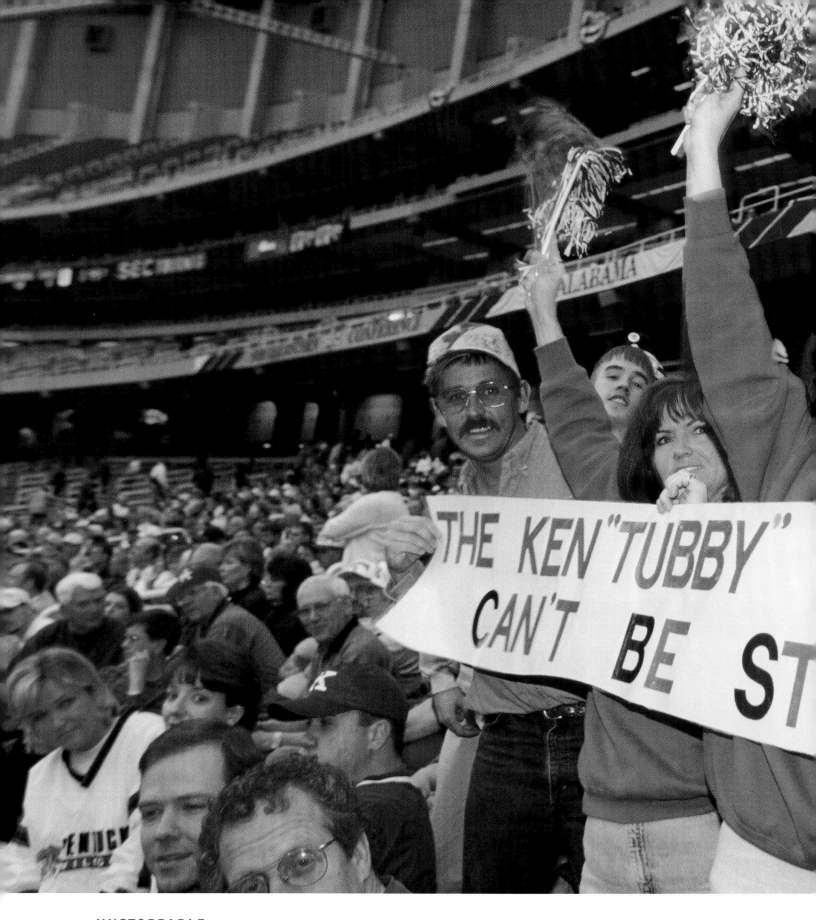

UNSTOPPABLE

**Calvin & Tammy Blanton & Jana M. Alvey of Lynchfield, Kentucky, &
Patricia Gallagher of Caneyville, Kentucky**

LICENSE TO THRILL

This started years ago. I'd been a fan for some time, but I really got caught up in it in '96 when they won the National Championship. I had followed them all year and never dreamed they'd end up in New York at the Final Four, but they did. I'm not the only one who dresses up—I've got a lot of friends who do, too. It's almost become a competition to see who can dress up the best. I'm also a Kentucky football fan, it's a year-round thing for me. There's a small lull between basketball and football, but not much.

The license plate was bought for me by a friend. I started wearing it around my neck, and have really built up a kind of following. I always see people at tournaments who come up to me and say, "Hey, Joe," and I don't have any idea who they are. But they remember the license plate. People holler and scream and blow their horn at me. It's kinda neat. I never thought I'd become a celebrity. I'm just a huge Cats fan.

**"Kentucky" Joe Crain,
Stanford, Kentucky**

FURRY FAN

Elizabeth & Keith Johnson,
Louisville, Kentucky

CATLANTICS

Tommy Arnold, Keith Hampton, Matt Bell, & Wade Sholar,
Hopkinsville, Kentucky

HAIR-RAISING

Tara Tsioropoulos, Atlanta, Georgia, & Nancy Clark-Pickrel, Louisville, Kentucky

WIGGED WILDCATS

This is my cousin's sweater. She bought it at a consignment store for four dollars and it was the only thing she brought in her suitcase. But she gave it to me to wear for my first game. This is so much fun.

Sabrina Hackett of Atlanta, Georgia, with Edwin Siliezar of Falls Church, Virginia, & Jack Grubbs of Vine Grove, Kentucky

C-A-T-S
C-A-T-S
C-A-T-S
CATS! CATS! CATS!

Cheryl Kennedy, Tucker, Georgia, &
Andy Burton, Lilburn, Georgia

THE NASHVILLE CAT

I am a huge Kentucky fan who lives in Tennessee. You can imagine how difficult that can be! Folks come down on me pretty hard, but they know that we're also national champions.

Sometimes my wife gets on me about my closet. I have white things on white hangers and blue things on blue hangers. And that's all. But she still tells me to get organized. What's to organize? It's all blue and white!

Randy Batey, Nashville, Tennessee

WHOOSH!

Randy Batey,
Nashville, Tennessee

PAINT BY
NUMBER ONE

**Andrew Katen &
Nick Gold, Lexington,
Kentucky, &
Jared Geis, New
Orleans, Louisiana**

CATMAN

Todd Brown,
Atlanta, Georgia

MAMA CATS

Lisa Longino & Sheila Fralick,
Louisville, Kentucky

FACES IN THE CROWD

Shane Wagner, Amy C. Goins, & Matt Felts,
Covington, Kentucky

MIRACLE MAN

Adam Miracle,
Lexington, Kentucky

BLUE MAN

Cordelia Schaber,
Villa Hills, Kentucky

CAT ATTIRE

Diane Haber,
lexington, Kentucky

TRUE-BLUE TOGAS

Nell Marie Merrick, Ashley Hill,
& Sheila Byron of Grand Rivers,
Kentucky, & Jason Adams of
Atlanta, Georgia

TRUE BLUE, THROUGH
AND THROUGH . . .

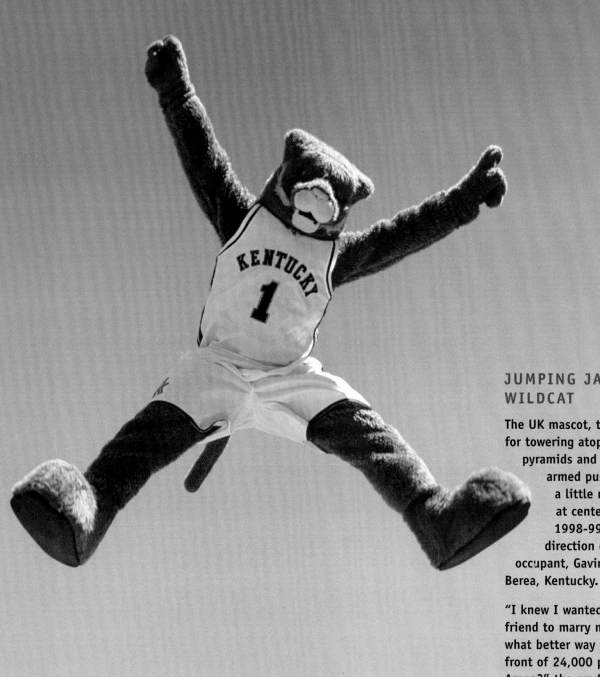

JUMPING JACK WILDCAT

The UK mascot, traditionally known for towering atop rotating human pyramids and executing one-armed push-ups, generated a little more excitement at center court during the 1998-99 season under the direction of its three-year occupant, Gavin Lee Duerson of Berea, Kentucky.

"I knew I wanted to ask my girl-friend to marry me, and I thought, what better way to do it than in front of 24,000 people in Rupp Arena?" the graduating lovesick senior purred. "It was quite a big event. I even had our parents there. Right before we got ready to do the pyramid I put on a T-shirt that said, 'Karla, will you marry me?' The people in front immediately realized what was going on, but she was over in the end zone and didn't see it at first. Everyone was cheering, and when we finally rotated to face her seat, her mouth dropped and she started to freak out. The cheerleaders, who were all in on it, got her up and walked her out to center court. I proposed to her right there and carried her off the floor."

THE RINGS

I have three National Championship rings. I only wear two because it looks a little hokey to put the third one on. I haven't found any way that I could really wear them all. I've tried.

(He wears '78 and '98. '96 is hidden away in his desk.)

**"Mr. Wildcat" Bill Keightley,
Lexington, Kentucky**

THE MAN

The acceptance and response I've had from the fans since I've been here has been overwhelming. Fans identify with Kentucky basketball more so than they do with anything else because of the great tradition, which is something that goes all the way back, even before Adolph Rupp. It's a way of life around here—something that people can hang their hat on. Something people feel they can count on year in and year out. And I'm one of those guys who likes to get out and shake people's hands. I want to meet as many people as I can around this state. I think that has drawn me closer and given me a greater appreciation of the fans and of Kentuckians.

The fans do so many wonderful things. I could go on and on with the many ways they show their concern and their care for Kentucky basketball and the team, but one of the best things is they follow us everywhere we go.

When we come out and see that we have so many fans, it makes us want to play a lot harder.

Orlando "Tubby" Smith,
Head Coach, Kentucky Wildcat
Basketball Team

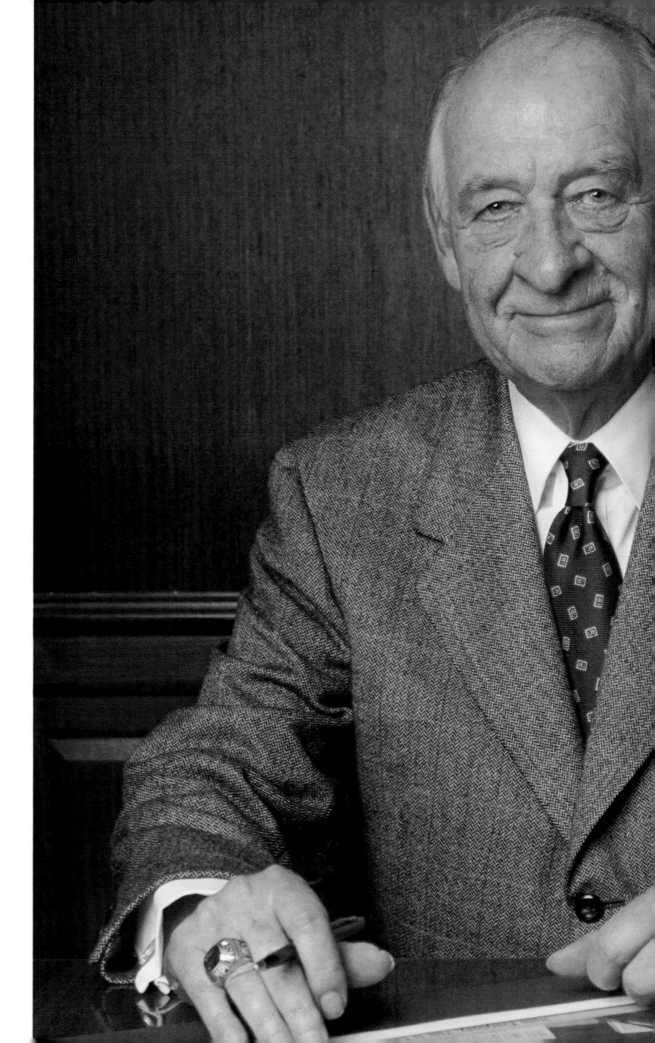

THE VOICE

I think Kentucky fans follow their team more closely than any other team in college basketball. No matter where we play, fans pack the place, and I think that gives UK somewhat of an edge.

At Ole Miss, which is not too far from Western Kentucky, the Kentucky following got so big that the university ticket office would not fill any ticket requests with a Kentucky postmark. And at Tennessee, we took more fans to Knoxville than the Volunteers had in Knoxville.

What else is incredible is that when people move from Kentucky to another state with its own team, they stay loyal to the University of Kentucky, because that's where they grew up. Some of those fans teach their children to root for the Wildcats and to be Kentucky fans, even if they have never been to the Bluegrass State.

That's a bit amazing.

**Cawood Ledford,
Lexington, Kentucky**

THE LEGEND

Not to sound like I'm bragging by any means, but when I came out of high school, I had over nine-hundred scholarship offers, and the fans were the reason why I opted to come to the University of Kentucky. They always said basketball was a way of life in the Bluegrass State. Not until I was here did I realize just how important it really is. The fans' primary concern throughout their lives is how the Kentucky Wildcats are going to do each season. It's the ultimate dream for anyone born in this state to put on a Kentucky uniform and play at Rupp Arena. It is second to none.

In my career I've had the opportunity to play against a lot of the greats, like Isaiah Thomas, Magic Johnson, and Shaquille; but whomever I might be talking to, everyone always asks, "What was it like to play for the University of Kentucky?" It is such a powerful institution that NBA All-Stars making millions of dollars a year want to know about my college basketball experience.

Sam Bowie
Lexington, Kentucky

1998 MIDNIGHT MADNESS

KENTUCKY

Photo: David Coyle

LET THE MADNESS BEGIN . . .

Because NCAA regulations state that players cannot officially begin practicing until October 15, and because Wildcats fans don't want to wait a second longer than absolutely necessary to see their "Boys in Blue," the team takes to the floor of the Memorial Coliseum at a few seconds past midnight each year to welcome the fans back, and vice versa, Kentucky-style.

The anticipation just keeps building. Everybody is so hungry for the season to begin and to see the team in their uniforms, because we know that it's about to start all over again. We know that once this night is here, we can pull out all of our team gear and get going. We usually get there early. They have things going on from about 8:30 or 9, and continue to build it up until the team hits the floor. When it's time, they make the stadium dark, then up come the lights and music and thunder . . . it's very dramatic. People eat it up. They go crazy.

**Robin Crain,
Stanford, Kentucky**

**Tubby Smith, dressed as Don King,
Midnight Madness 1998**

MIDNIGHT MADNESS
. . . ATLANTA STYLE

Bill Keightley hands over the sweaty uniforms to an anxious Diana Shelton of Marietta, Georgia

The equipment manager Bill Keightley called three years ago and said, "Diana, where's David?" I told him that my husband was down at the SEC tournament. And he said, "Well, then tell me, where is the nearest laundromat? I have to wash the uniforms tonight and get them back in the morning." I told him, "If I knew where there was one, I wouldn't send you to it in downtown Atlanta in the middle of the night, because we'd never see you again. It's really dangerous." I told him to meet me in the lobby after the game and I'd pick them up and wash them at home. It was 10:00 at night when I picked up the wash. I had all this company visiting from out of town and my husband was down at the game. Then he called and asked, "What are you doing?" And I replied, "David, you will not believe what I'm doing. I am washing the Wildcats' uniforms." Well, he came to life. He rushed home, found Jeff Shepard's uniform in the pile of wet clothes, put it on, and went out in the driveway and started shooting baskets at 1:00 in the morning.

And now every year Bill says he knows he doesn't have to worry because I'll wash the uniforms and get them back to the team by the next morning. I enjoy this, I really do. I look forward to it every year. We've heard from so many people who want me to retell the story and they always say, "Well, how did you get this job?" And I have to explain to them that I am not the "Laundry Lady of Atlanta," I'm just the laundry lady for UK when they play in Atlanta and need clean uniforms the next day. I always have people offering to help, but I have to say no because I think, "What if?"

**Diana Shelton,
Marietta, Georgia**

MARCH 12, 1977

FOREVER A FAN

I have been to over 1,100 Kentucky basketball games since my first game in the Alumni Gym in 1944. I was sixteen years old, and we played the Illinois Whiz Kids. They were a pretty good team and had beaten us in Illinois, but when they came to Kentucky, we returned the favor.

I had attended 615 consecutive games before I had a heart attack and had to miss 4 games during the Alaska Shootout. I was all packed and ready to go when I woke up that morning with chest pains. I went to the hospital and am really glad I wasn't on that airplane. Now I'm back to over one hundred consecutive games attended.

Out of all my memories as a fan, winning the national championship has been my favorite. We've won seven and I've been fortunate enough to see four of them— '58, '78, '96, and '98. I don't do anything else. I will never retire from Kentucky basketball. I still wear a coat and tie to every game, and I plan on doing this until I just can't do it anymore.

Bill Wiggins,
Falmouth, Kentucky

CATS-EYE VIEW

For me, the mania started when I was young. Ever since I can remember I've loved Kentucky basketball, and have always collected Wildcat stuff like crazy. Dad and Mom always gave me stuff—some of it is over twenty-five years old. About three years after we bought this house, I decided to add on a room to hold it all. It was just an open area taking up space, so I figured I'd turn it into a place to watch the ball games when I'm not there in person.

Johnny Walters

Johnny keeps buying me keychains, so I just keep on hooking them together. I carry them everywhere I go. People say I'm going to tear up my ignition, but I say no, it's tough as a Wildcat. The dress is one Johnny bought for me in Lexington. It's a kid's size but it fits me. Now I'm thinking about getting a permanent blue streak in my hair.

La Donna Walters

Johnny & La Donna Walters, with their daughter Megan & son Johnathan, Campbellsville, Kentuck

TEE TIME, WILDCAT-STYLE

After we won the '98 championship, I thought that the people who live around our summer home, and are mainly from Ohio, needed to be more aware of the happenings in the Bluegrass State. So I decided to decorate my golf cart in celebration of the victory. It took about a week to meticulously mask all the rubber, and then I spray-painted it Wildcat blue. Some friends helped me accumulate the various decals and stickers that adorn it. Then I added the Kentucky fight song to play when someone makes a good shot. One thing about my golf cart, no one has a problem locating me on the course!

"Ranger Bob,"
Robert H. Owens,
Crestview Hills, Kentucky

"RANGER BOB" TALKS ABOUT . . .

The blue pants I've had for twelve years now, and I could have sold them about one hundred times. I designed them myself. I was in the bookstore and saw all of these patches and thought they would look neat on a pair of pants. So I bought a bunch of them and laid them out the way I wanted, and then my wife sewed them on. I also have a pair for football and a pair of winter corduroys.

I think Kentucky fans are the greatest fans in the world. I've also heard it said that Kentucky athletics is like a religion in this state, and I think it's essentially true. If you've toured our state then you know that we have some really depressed areas, and the only thing a lot of people had to look forward to on the weekends was listening to Cawood Ledford broadcast football and basketball games. So not only do I take it as a religion, I take it personally. If someone bad-mouths the University of Kentucky, it's like they're talking about someone in my family, and I believe that's the consensus of many fans throughout the state.

"Ranger Bob"

OAY BUFFET

ORBACK SALAD

MECOCK STEW

ATOR TAIL

IGER MEAT

AWG BONES

A HORSE OF A DIFFERENT COLOR

Wildcat Blue is a Thoroughbred mare belonging to Mike Sloan. He sent her here to the farm and asked that we name her. We wanted to name her something Blue because her sire is Cure The Blues. At that time, Kentucky was in the NCAA finals and won. That cinched it— we named her Wildcat Blue. When you're born and raised in Kentucky you've got to like the Wildcats. There's just not another team.

**Robert S. McMillin,
Wildcat Blue & her foal,
Georgetown, Kentucky**

I DON'T THINK YOU BECOME A KENTUCKY FAN . . . I THINK YOU'RE *BORN* A KENTUCKY FAN.

I grew up here in Nicholasville, which is only about ten miles south of the football stadium and Rupp Arena, so I went to my share of games as a kid. I still try to go when I'm not on the road. Of course my parents and everyone else's parents always watched Kentucky on TV, so I did the same way, following in their footsteps. And now I'm teaching my children what they taught me—Kentucky is the best place in the world. We just grew up being proud of the Wildcats. I don't think you become a Kentucky fan, I think you're *born* a Kentucky fan.

John Michael Montgomery,
Nicholasville, Kentucky

CAT COLLECTOR

I've been following the team since the late '60s, but really started collecting about five years ago. I bought one or two items and then my friends started giving me Wildcat stuff for Christmas. My favorite thing by far is my Rick Pitino autographed basketball. My second favorite is a book autographed by Adolph Rupp. Then a book autographed by Pat Riley. And of course my Ronald Mercer jersey is a favorite also. I know a lot of really big fans who might have four or five collector's items and a few shirts, but there aren't too many people who will collect hundreds of things like myself.

**Mike Tooley,
Brentwood, Tennessee**

WAXING BLUE

The now-famous blue-waxed bottle did not start with the championship. It started with a box of blue wax. One year, Governor John Y. Brown asked me to do the seal for his Derby invitations. We had to order a whole box of royal blue wax and used just a very small portion of it for the invites. Rather than throw the rest of it away, I just set it aside. When Rick (Pitino) had the team in comeback in 1993 and they had won the SEC Championship, I said, "Stop the bottling line, let's use the blue wax right now." And so we just did it as a joke and sent the bottles only to Lexington. Then I left town, and the blue-waxed bottle created quite a frenzy because there were only a couple thousand bottles and everyone wanted one. I thought C. M. Newton was going to kill me because demand for the bottle completely jammed UK's phone lines. Everyone was calling for the bottle. He finally phoned me and said, "Son, I'm not in the whisky business, could you tell these people that?"

When it looked like Kentucky was going to win the National Championship in 1996, I decided that we would do a special bottle again. Because we had created such a mess the first time, I planned to make enough bottles for everyone who wanted one. All of the profits would be donated to The Daniel Pitino Foundation, the charity Rick had started in remembrance of his late son. This became the bottle with the white wax and the blue denim label, which we did to poke subtle fun at Rick for that year's uniform fiasco. He had designed them thinking he was as good a uniform designer as he was a coach.

Bill Samuels Jr.,
President,
Maker's Mark Distillery, Inc.,
Louisville, Kentucky

Bill Samuels Jr., photographed at home in Prospect, Kentucky, entertained guests at his annual Derby party by dressing as Elton John.

RUPP-LICA

We built this gym to have a place for our ten kids to play. We wanted to know where they were on Friday and Saturday nights. Originally, it was going to be a half-court gym, but the kids talked me into making it full regulation size. They go to a school where the colors are red and black, so we had a little discussion about what color the gym should be painted. And blue and white won out, easily. After it was finished we named it "Rupp Arena North." It has the UK emblem at center court, blue padding all the way around, and "Kentucky Wildcats" painted on both ends.

Every kid in Northern Kentucky knows us, that's for sure. At the time we built the gym, I was scared that no one would use it, but it's been quite the contrary. We have games going on in here 365 days a year. During basketball season, there are sometimes three teams a day practicing here. It's really worked out well transportation-wise. Rather than take my ten kids to practice, the practice comes to the kids.

**Ted Arlinghaus,
Edgewood, Kentucky**

AND I'VE NEVER EVEN
LIVED IN KENTUCKY!

ORIGINAL CATS

I have always been a basketball fan.

I grew up in a basketball family. But I've been a UK fan for about forty years because my husband went to school there. My Wildcat collection started when we moved back to Frankfort twenty-six years ago.

I decided to make a sweatsuit that had everything on it about UK that I loved. So of course I put on a basketball. Then I added a heart to show how much I love UK, the words "Kentucky Wildcats," and of course, paw prints. Plus it's fully washable! I also made a purse that I carry to every game, a tissue box that says "National Champions" around the top, and a jewelry bag to hold all of my UK jewelry. There's even a pair of Wildcat earrings made for me by my granddaughter. My son Richard crocheted the pillow doll and sewed the cat. My oldest son painted the ceramic blue bear. The mouse and the UK nut were made for me by friends. I guess what makes my Wildcat collection so special is that each are handmade one-of-a-kind pieces that friends were nice enough to create for me.

**Billie Sue Abbott,
Frankfort, Kentucky**

HOME IS WHERE THE CATS ARE

This is our new RV. We've only had it for a year. Last year we went to the Final Four and traveled with the Cats for a month. We kept going from one town to another in a thirty-footer without a slide-out extender. When we got home I said, "Harold, I really need more space to put Kentucky Wildcat stuff in!" So we went out and got this one.

**Betty & Harold Browning,
Lancaster, Kentucky**

CAT HAVEN

We bought our first RV in '83 and started going to some of the games. Since I've retired we now have time to make the basketball tournament route. We just go as far as we can drive the Big Blue RV.

Bill Hackett,
Bethlehem, Kentucky

One nice thing about traveling with the Cats is that you meet so many people you would have never met had you not been a fan. I never believed we'd be able to travel like this. Never ever. But my husband worked hard for thirty-six years so that we could retire this way. It's a dream come true.

Joyce Hackett,
Bethlehem, Kentucky

PULLING FOR KENTUCKY

The locomotive originally was painted to raise awareness at train crossings and hopefully reduce accidents. We felt that people would be more on the lookout for locomotives if they had something to look for. The theme was, "Look out for your team locomotive," which we thought would appeal to everyone, even kids. This way, when they got to a train crossing, they would look both ways before crossing in hopes that they would see the Big Blue rolling up the track. It's bright and it catches your eye.

We did the car about five years ago, and at the time we were commemorating the last NCAA Championship, in '78. Now we're thinking about doing a couple more to commemorate '96 and '98 as well.

**Tony Reck,
President,
P & L Railroad,
Paducah, Kentucky**

"TRAINING" DOGS TO ROOT FOR CATS

So why am I sitting here in a UK robe next to a train? Because it reminds me of the first Kentucky basketball game I ever saw.

In the '50s, I boarded the Louisville & Nashville Railroad in Henderson for a cross-state trip to Louisville to see the SEC tournament.

Rupp was the coach, Cliff Hagan and Bobby Watson were two of their great players. Fortunately, I got my photo taken with both of them. Sadly, Kentucky lost the tournament. That explains the train.

The robe? That's another story. A dear lady friend of mine gave it to me because she loves me and I love her. I wear it for luck whenever I watch the Wildcats play on TV. Also, as any dog-equipped fan should do, I enlist support from my two guard beagles, Captain and Calhoun. The dogs never fail to give me a quizzical glance when I plead, "Okay, boys, it's time to root for the Cats!"

Gerry Wood,
author & UK graduate,
Nashville, Tennessee

QUIET CAT

I became a true fan at the age of ten. All my uncles would sit around and listen to Kentucky basketball on the radio, and if you couldn't be quiet, then you couldn't be in the room while the game was on. So at the age of ten I got to where I could be quiet enough, and that's when I started listening to Cawood. I've stayed with it ever since. It's a religion in Kentucky, being a fan of the Wildcats. The whole state is like a family. Everywhere you go, if you're wearing a Kentucky shirt or cap, people will come up and say, "What did you think of the game last night?" Even if you've never seen them before in your life, it's like you're talking to an old friend.

**Greg Mays,
Burlington, Kentucky**

Handpainted mural by Jerry Mainous

Items from the souvenir collection
of Greg Mays

A PIECE OF HISTORY

A friend of mine, David Bailey, was at Memorial Coliseum doing some repair work on the floor, which had sustained some water damage. They had to take up some of the old floor, so he cut off a piece and gave it to me.

**Greg Mays,
Burlington, Kentucky**

HARROD CONCRETE
FRANKFORT, KENTUCKY

With over fifty years invested in the University of Kentucky, Bill Harrod and his sons, Stuart and David, have a deep love for the Big Blue. They even had toy cement trucks made and painted blue and white for the kids and grandchildren.

"Being a Kentucky Wildcat fan is the law in our family," David chimes. "I was six years old when my dad took me to my first game. We drove from Louisville to Lexington and I've been going ever since. I can't tell you if we won or lost but I do remember the drive back and forth, where we stopped to eat, the whole nine yards. We follow basketball, football, baseball, the ladies' swim team . . . if it's blue and white, we're for it."

"The one thing I remember about graduating high school is that everybody else in my class was traveling around the country deciding where they wanted to go to college," adds Stuart. "I knew from the beginning where I was headed. I was going to the University of Kentucky. That was it. End of discussion."

Stuart Harrod, David Harrod,
& their father Bill Harrod,
Frankfort, Kentucky

SET IN STONE

Our trucks have been painted blue and white since the beginning. This new logo is only a few years old, but we've always painted our trucks to look like footballs with laces painted on them, or with big pictures of the Wildcat. When the new logo came out we decided to paint it on all of our cement trucks, and had to get a license from the University to do so. Now we are proud to have a fleet of forty trucks showing off the Wildcat logo all over the great state of Kentucky.

William R. Harrod,
President,
Harrod Concrete and Stone Co.,
Frankfort, Kentucky

BLUE SUEDE SHOES

When I was little and had just started going to games, one of the things I really enjoyed was the ambience—all the crazy fans dressed up and the atmosphere it created. I never thought that one day I'd be one of those characters, but once you get started you can't stop. I started the Elvis thing five years ago when the tournament was in Memphis. It went so well that I kept it up. Now I dress up for all the tournament games, the SEC, the NCAA, and the Final Four. I travel everywhere the Wildcats go. If I quit, the peer pressure would kill me. Every year I add something. Last year I got a much better wig and these cool glasses. Now they're my trademark.

**Rick D. Cothern,
Bowling Green, Kentucky**

ONE ON ONE

Billie Sue & Keith Abbott,
Frankfort, Kentucky

CAT'S GOT HER TONGUE

Kentucky fan Jeff Thiemann asks Jen Smarr to become his wife with the help of the Wildcat mascot at Rupp Arena. "I had no idea what was going on," says Jen. "All I knew was the Cat was crawling all over the people in our aisle, making them miss the game. I was totally shocked." Naturally, she said yes.

Jack Cooley, Lexington, Kentucky

SEEING SPOTS

If I could really breed a dog with blue spots, I'd make a fortune.

Sidney Remmele, D.V.M., with his dalmatian, Vicki, Lexington, Kentucky

BILLY BLUE

There is no better fan in the world than one who gets choked up at the mention of the Wildcats. Such is the story with Bill Kirkland, who realized his obsession at a very young age. "I was seven years old when my dad took me to my first Kentucky ballgame. We were sitting in the stands and he said, 'There are no two better colors together than blue and white.' "

A graduate of the University of Kentucky, he and his wife actively participate in the Kentucky Athletic program by sponsoring a cheerleader each semester with a scholarship. A member of several organizations on and off campus, this incredible fan still does not have season tickets to Rupp Arena. "It's the toughest ticket in sports. Tougher than the Derby. Just a really hard ticket to get," he says with a smile.

"The plaque is one of Cawood Ledford's stat sheets. He did the lettering by hand, all of it. It's even been signed by him. It occupies THE spot in my blue room; it's my favorite thing. He's a great guy. A special guy. A real Kentucky treasure."

Bill Kirkland,
Lexington, Kentucky

138

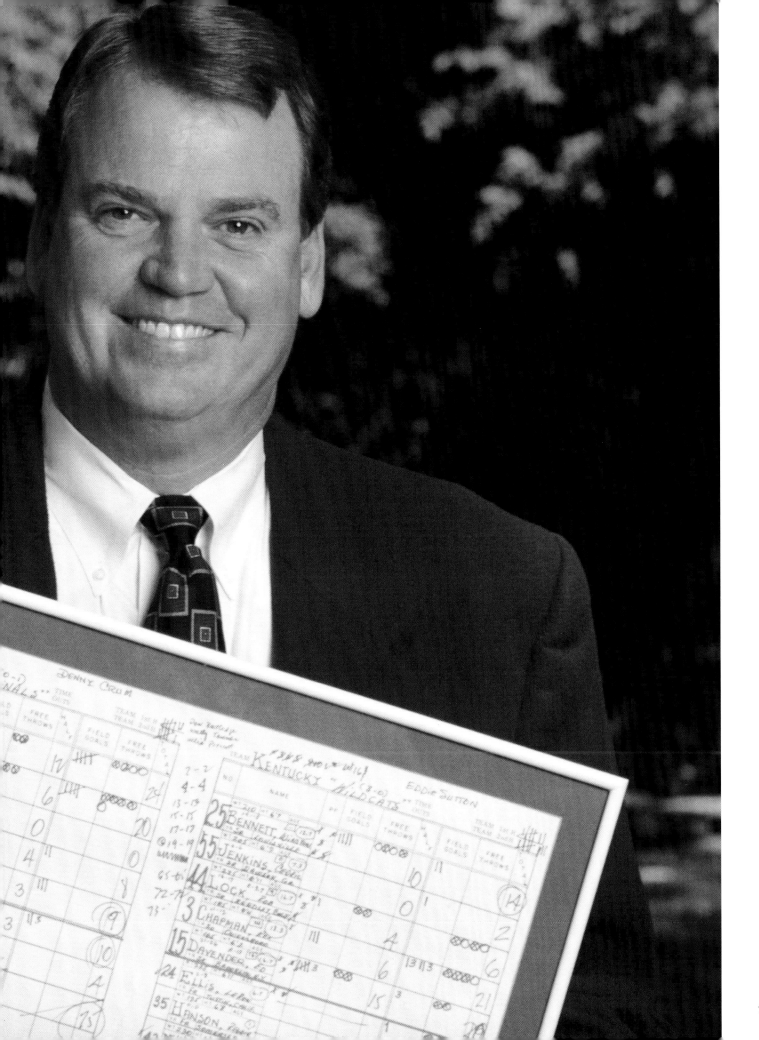

139

BALANCING ACT

WVLK was the flagship station for the Wildcats when Eddie Sutton resigned. Then came the search for a new coach, and not just anyone could be the coach of Kentucky. To support the search, our general manager, Ralph Hacker, came up with the idea for someone to go up on a billboard and stay up there until a new coach was named. "Wild-eyed Wildcat" was the theme. At the time, I was the only one physically able to do it because we had no idea how long it would take—one month, six months, we didn't know. All we knew was that we were committed to stay up there until a new coach had signed a contract.

So up I went May 10, 1989. It was amazing how it grew and grew, almost by the hour, because it was so unique at the time. A furniture store donated a Lazy Boy, a cable company hooked me up with cable, a coffee place brought me coffee every morning. I can still close my eyes and hear the horns going off.

Relieved is what I was when I got to come down. The toughest part was Coach Pitino was still in the playoffs with the Knicks and refused to talk about Kentucky until they were over. I would see him on TV and he would poo-poo the whole thing.

His first stop on the day he came to town—June 1, 1989— was to my billboard. He said, "I just want you to know, I'm going to get you off here tomorrow," so I sent him a telegram telling him I would give him anything if he'd just accept the job. And he did. So down I came. I hadn't shaved in three weeks. I looked like a cave man.

But given the same set of circumstances today, I'd probably do it again. It's like Kentucky is the Roman Empire of college basketball, you know?

Robert Lindsey,
WVLK Radio,
Lexington, Kentucky

ALL FOR NUMBER ONE

I wanted my room to be blue and white because I like the Wildcats a whole lot. I haven't been to a game yet, but after the championship game I handed my mom the car keys and made her drive me around so I could hang out the window and flash the lights and beep the horn.

Patrick Lindsey allows little brother Jason & his parents, Eileen & Robert, into his cool blue & white room for a quick family portrait.

AMBASSADOR FOR
WILDCAT COUNTRY

I became a fan before I was able to talk. My dad and I would listen to games, and back during that time, Kentuckians didn't have much else to talk about. Then I went into the service and kids from New Jersey and New York could not believe that I was from Kentucky, because I didn't have much of a twang. Out in the world that was the perception of what Kentucky was all about. But we've always been a beautiful state with a fantastic basketball program. It was and is something to be proud of, something people talk about, something that the state is noted for.

The license plate is a special edition pewter plate that they made in '78 after winning the national championship. It's 101 of only 1,000 plates made. It lives on my sunshiny-day car, a '94 Corvette.

Gene Courtney, with his wife Gayle & their dog, Baron von Courtney, Florence, Kentucky

THE THRONE OF VICTORY

I was off work for seven months and got really bored, so I decided to paint my bathroom, even though I had no art training at all. It had floral wallpaper in it so I painted three coats of white paint first and then got started on the fun part. I went to the craft store and got little bitty paint brushes and literally used toothpicks to do a lot of the detail stuff. It took all that time to get it to where it is today and it's one of those things that's a never-ending story. My husband Gene said that when we move we should cut the drywall out and take it with us, because the people who move in might not be UK fans, and they'll paint over the top of it and it will be gone. I would really hate that.

Gayle Courtney,
Florence, Kentucky

LOVE THOSE CATS

I've been a Wildcats fan my whole
life. I love Tubby Smith and I think
the boys will do great this year and
every year. Go Big Blue!

**Steve McBee,
Florence, Kentucky**

LONGTIME FAN

I have been to four of the last seven NCAA Championships. Kentucky has won seven total and I have been present at the '68, '78, '96, and '98 games. There are only two others that I know of who can say that. My favorite moment was the '59 championship, because that team, the "Fiddling Five," as Rupp called them, weren't supposed to win. Back then you only needed four wins where now you need six, and all four were played in the state of Kentucky. The first two rounds were in Lexington Memorial Coliseum and the final two were in Louisville. I was in college at UK at the time and I drove to Louisville with nineteen dollars in my pocket, that's all. There was a fellow selling tickets outside and for two five-dollar tickets, he wanted twenty dollars. I told him I only had nineteen and he took it. So we had no money for anything else, not even a drink. But we got to see the game.

Jerry Stricker,
Covington, Kentucky

BIGG BLUE MARTINI

Before they opened the bar, there was a promotion for the Bigg Blue martini creation. Bartenders around the city were asked to come in and make their martini. They were to be judged on quality of drink, presentation, and crowd support. The winner would become the Bigg Blue Mixologist and be recognized as the creator of the best martini in Lexington. So Brian and I got together—he was my crew chief and technical advisor—and we went for it. We showed up, mixed our drink, and won. Part of my presentation was mixing the drink on one of those old exercise machines called "The Jiggler." Maybe that sealed the deal.

Ray's Blue Jiggler

- 3 jiggers of Absolut vodka, shaken over ice
- 1 $1/2$ jiggers of blue curaçao
- 1 splash each of lime juice, triple sec, & sour mix
- pour into martini glass with a blue sugar rim
- garnish with a blue gelatin cube or blue gumdrops

Bigg Blue martini creator, W. R. "Ray" Collins, & his crew chief & technical advisor, Brian Lamar, put the finishing touches on their masterpiece at the Bigg Blue Martini in Lexington, Kentucky.

CAT'S MEOW

We both grew up in the bluegrass. I went to UK for a while. You automatically become a Wildcat fan when you're born and raised in Kentucky.—**Troy**

I'm sure there are photos of me as a newborn with a Kentucky basketball in my hands. That's the first toy my dad gave me. Being a Wildcat fan is a genetic thing. If you're born in Kentucky, you're a fan. And if you're from out of state and live in Kentucky for a year, you start covering yourself in blue and yelling, "Go, Cats!"—**Eddie**

When we are on the road and a UK basketball game comes on—and we can't pick it up on our bus satellite dish—we head to the nearest sports bar. Sometimes we might be a little late for our next gig, but we don't care. UK comes first!—**Troy**

As much as we love music, Kentucky basketball is right up there on the same level. Like all Kentucky fans, we really get involved in the games. When they lose, you feel like you've lost your best friend. It just rips your heart out. That loss is hard to swallow. But when they win, you're soaring!—**Eddie**

**Eddie Montgomery & Troy Gentry
of the group Montgomery Gentry,
Lexington, Kentucky**

CAT'S ENTERTAINMENT

I've always been a UK fanatic. I grew up with it. I can't remember not having a basketball. I was always out in the backyard dribbling like all Kentucky boys do. I would play at night—shoot in the dark and then come inside and listen to Clyde Sullivan (pre-Cawood Ledford days)—and that was just my idea of heaven.

My dad had a passion for Kentucky basketball as well, and he was always very supportive of me. In Kentucky you follow the Cats. There are no professional sports and everyone loves the Big Blue. So when we moved to Georgia, my wife and both of my daughters wanted to surprise me with something I'd really like. So for Father's Day, they had this bar put in. I was definitely shocked. We have a great time, all my buddies gather around the bar and we listen to the games and have a cold beverage or two. We probably listen to more games than we watch. It's a lot of fun. Kentucky basketball is a happening and I honestly don't know what I would do without it.

David Shelton,
Marietta, Georgia

THANKS FOR SHARING

Ken Duncan & Carla Perkins of Nashville, Tennessee, help David Sands celebrate his first UK basketball game by sharing their homemade sign with him & his mother Catherine, both of Decatur, Georgia.

KENTUCKY
INVITATIONAL
1999
anks for Playing
ee You Next Year

YOU CAN TAKE IT
WITH YOU

We had a family come in needing to purchase a casket for their father. He had been a big UK fan from way back, and to honor that passion, his family wanted a casket with blue and white accessories. After doing a bit of research, I discovered that our company could get an authentic University of Kentucky casket. The family was overwhelmed. They were so happy to be able to make this final gesture that they cried.

Marsha DeHaven,
President,
Consumers Choice Monuments
and Caskets,
Louisville, Kentucky

"If you lead a good life, go to Sunday School and Church, say your prayers every night, when you die you'll go to Kentucky."